Egypt

In the Past and Present

John Perritano

◄ Egypt has a long history. This statue was made more than 4,000 years ago.

Contents

BOOK DESIGN/PHOTO RESEARCH
Steve Curtis Design, Inc.

Copyright © 2006 National Geographic Society.
All Rights Reserved. Reproduction of the whole or any part of the
contents without written permission from the publisher is prohibited.
National Geographic, National Geographic School Publishing,
National Geographic Reading Expeditions, and the Yellow Border
are registered trademarks of the National Geographic Society.

Published by the National Geographic Society
1145 17th Street N.W.
Washington, D.C. 20036-4688

ISBN-13: 978-0-7922-5465-2
ISBN-10: 0-7922-5465-1

2014
    4 5 6 7 8 9 10 11 12 13 14 15

Printed in Canada.

Where Is Egypt?

Egypt is a country in northeastern Africa. Near Egypt, three continents or large landmasses come together. The continents are Europe, Asia, and Africa.

Most of Egypt is a desert. The land is hot and dry. Yet the world's longest river runs through Egypt. This river is called the Nile.

The Nile River is a source of water for people in Egypt. People need water to live. So the Nile River gives life to Egypt. The river has helped people live in Egypt for 5,000 years.

Egypt

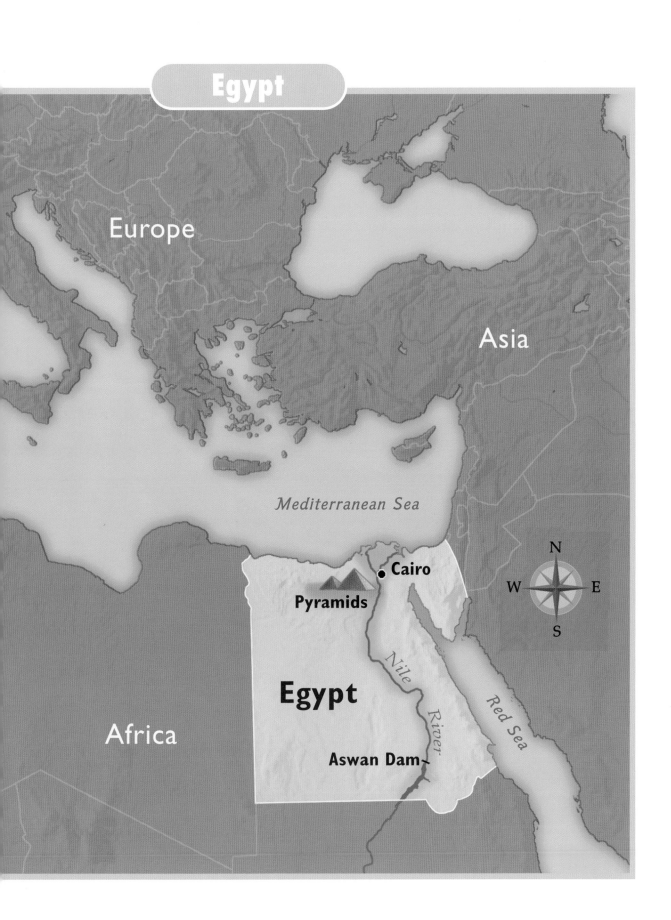

Egypt

Europe

Asia

Mediterranean Sea

Cairo

Pyramids

Egypt

Africa

Nile River

Red Sea

Aswan Dam

N
W   E
S

Ancient

Big Idea
The ancient Egyptians created one of the world's first great civilizations.

Set Purpose
Read to learn what life was like in ancient Egypt.

▼ The ancient Egyptians built this temple about 3,000 years ago.

Questions You Will Explore

Who were the ancient Egyptians?
What was life like in ancient Egypt?

Egyptians

Egypt was home to one of the first great **civilizations.** The people of ancient Egypt lived 5,000 years ago. Yet they invented a system of writing. They created a calendar much like ours. They also built amazing things from stone. Who were these ancient Egyptians?

civilization – a highly developed culture

The Nile River

The ancient Egyptians lived along the Nile River. People drank the river's water. They used it to cook and bathe. They caught fish in the river. They traveled in boats on the river, too.

Each year, the Nile River flooded. The flood left a thick strip of black **silt** behind. That silt made the land good for farming. It helped Egyptians live.

....
silt – a deposit of fresh soil

▼ The Nile River today looks much like it did long ago.

Farming in Egypt

The Egyptians planted many **crops.** They grew barley and wheat for bread. They planted leeks, beans, and cabbage to eat. They grew flax to make into cloth.

The Egyptians needed water for their crops. So they dug canals. These canals brought water from the Nile to the fields. In this way, Egyptians could water their crops.

....
crop – a plant that is grown to be used

▼ **Many ancient Egyptians farmed the land.**

Egyptian Homes

The ancient Egyptians learned how to make bricks from straw and mud. They used these bricks to build homes. Most houses had only one room. But some homes had two or three stories. People sometimes slept on the roof during the summer to keep cool. They covered windows and doors with mats. The mats kept out insects and dust.

▼ This drawing shows how some Egyptians might have lived long ago.

Egyptian Clothes

It was hot in Egypt. So people wore light clothes to keep cool. The clothes had a loose fit. Men wore a short skirt called a kilt. Women wore dresses held up by straps. People usually walked barefoot. They wore sandals only for special events.

▼ These are sandals from ancient Egypt.

▼ This ancient painting shows how some people dressed.

11

The Pharaoh

A king, or **pharaoh,** was the ruler of ancient Egypt. The pharaoh was very powerful. Ancient Egyptians believed he was a god. They obeyed his every word.

The pharaoh had large armies. The pharaoh also had many **slaves.** These slaves plowed the pharaoh's fields and did his heavy work.

pharaoh – an ancient Egyptian king

slave – a person who is forced to work without pay

◀ **This gold mask was made in honor of a young pharaoh.**

Building Pyramids

The ancient Egyptians built **pyramids** of heavy stone. Pharaohs were buried inside when they died. No one knows just how the pyramids were built. Some people think the Egyptians used sleds and other tools. The sleds helped people move the heavy stones. People dragged the stones up a ramp and into place.

....

pyramid – a building with four sides that come together to form a point

◀ The pyramids looked like this when they were done.

▼ Pyramids may have been built with ramps and sleds.

Many Gods

The ancient Egyptians believed in many gods and goddesses. Their main god was Ra, the sun god. Ra and the goddess Rennutet brought good harvests. The most important goddess was Isis. Egyptians worshiped Isis as the protector of the dead.

◀ The god Ra had the head of a falcon, or hunting bird.

Life After Death

The ancient Egyptians believed in life after death. They took care of important people who had died. They treated dead bodies with oils and herbs. Then they wrapped the bodies in cloth. Today, we call these bodies **mummies.**

Egyptians put their mummies into tombs. Then they filled the tombs with gold and jewelry. Modern scientists have found many tombs and mummies. They study these things to learn how ancient Egyptians lived.

....

mummy – a dead body that is treated and wrapped in cloth to make it last a long time

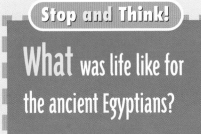

Stop and Think!

What was life like for the ancient Egyptians?

▼ **After this mummy was made, it was covered in gold.**

Egyptian Life Today

Recap
Describe how the
ancient Egyptians
worked and lived.

Set Purpose
Discover what
Egyptian life is
like today.

Egypt today is a mix of ancient and modern ways. The streets of Cairo are full of cars and trucks. But they are crowded with camels and donkey carts, too. Modern stores sell computers and TVs. Yet people still buy from the ancient bazaar, or marketplace. Modern buildings stand near an ancient pyramid.

▼ Modern and ancient are side by side in Egypt today.

Life Along the Nile

Many people in Egypt still live along the Nile River. As in ancient times, some women still wash their clothes in the river. Some men still fish along its banks. The Nile is still used for **transport,** too. Small boats carry people up and down the river. Huge boats carry food, oil, and other cargo to distant countries.

....

transport – a way of moving people or things

▲ **The Nile River is still important to Egyptian life today.**

Farming Today

Today, there are fewer farms along the Nile River. The river does not flood anymore. So the soil is not as rich as it used to be. The land is harder to farm. Farmers must now spread fertilizer to grow good crops. But farmers still rely on the Nile to water their crops. Many farms are larger than in ancient times.

▼ **Modern farming is hard work, just as in ancient times.**

Modern Homes

Egypt has many large cities. People live in modern houses and apartments. They have refrigerators and stoves. They have air-conditioning. Some houses even have pools.

In the countryside, houses are more like those of long ago. There, buildings are still made from mud brick. Some houses have electricity and running water. Other houses do not.

▼ **This is Cairo, the capital of Egypt.**

Kids in Egypt

Egyptian kids share much in common with kids in the United States. They eat pizza and ice cream. Some kids wear T-shirts and cargo pants. Kids talk on cell phones. They enjoy movies. They like to hang out. Just as in the United States, Egyptian kids also go to school.

▼ Kids play a game in front of an ancient temple.

The Economy Today

Tourism is very important in Egypt today. People come from all over the world to see the sights. They visit the temples and tombs along the Nile. They take tours down the river.

Tourism brings many jobs to the region. Thousands of people work in hotels and restaurants. Many work as bus drivers or tour guides.

....

tourism – the visiting of a place by people from somewhere else

▼ **Tourism is important to the Egyptian economy today.**

Egypt's Past and Present

Egypt's past has long fascinated the world. People come to see the pyramids. They come to learn about life in this ancient land. In Egypt today, the past is always present.

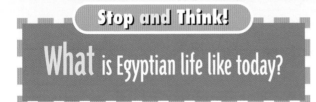

Stop and Think!

What is Egyptian life like today?

▼ A young Egyptian learns about his country's ancient culture.

Recap
Describe what life is like in Egypt today.

Set Purpose
Read more about life in ancient Egypt.

CONNECT WHAT YOU HAVE LEARNED

Egypt in the Past and Present

Egypt was home to one of the world's first civilizations. The ancient Egyptians created one of the longest lasting cultures in history.

Here are some ideas that you learned about life in ancient Egypt.

- The ancient Egyptians lived and farmed along the Nile River.
- The ruler of ancient Egypt was called a pharaoh.
- The ancient Egyptians built pyramids and temples of stone.
- Egypt's past is still important today.

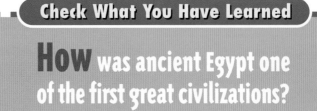

Check What You Have Learned

How was ancient Egypt one of the first great civilizations?

▲ The Nile was an important source of water.

▲ Pharaohs were wealthy and powerful rulers.

▲ Some Egyptian temples are thousands of years old.

▲ People come from around the world to learn about ancient Egypt.

▲ These are hieroglyphs, or word pictures.

Hieroglyphs

Ancient Egyptians used a form of picture writing. The pictures were called hieroglyphs. Hieroglyphs tell what life was like in ancient Egypt. They show rulers and celebrations. They also tell about daily events. Egyptians had more than 700 symbols for different sounds and letters.

▶ Today, people need help to read the ancient hieroglyphs.

The Rosetta Stone

For centuries, no one could read hieroglyphs. Then in 1799, French soldiers found a tablet near the town of Rosetta. The tablet is called the Rosetta stone.

The Rosetta stone shows the same message in three types of writing. One message was written in hieroglyphs. Another was written in ancient Greek. Historians compared the hieroglyphs to the Greek words. Finally, they could read what the ancient Egyptians had written.

▶ **The Rosetta stone is written in three languages.**

27

▲ **An Egyptian woman makes papyrus paper.**

Papyrus

▲ **Ancient writing on papyrus paper**

The ancient Egyptians invented a type of paper called papyrus. They made this paper from a plant that grew along the Nile River. People cut the stems off the plant. They sliced the stems into strips. Then they pounded the strips together to make a strong paper. Pieces of papyrus paper have lasted thousands of years.

Aswan Dam

In 1902, engineers built a dam in Egypt. The dam was near the town of Aswan. Farmers used water from the dam to water their fields. In 1970, people built a bigger dam in Aswan. This dam keeps the Nile from flooding. It stores water, too. The water helps people when there is not enough rain. The dam also uses water to make electricity. The dam is more than two miles long. It crosses from one side of the Nile to the other.

▼ The Aswan Dam

Many kinds of words are used in this book. Here you will learn about homophones. You will also learn about the past tense.

Homophones

Homophones are words that sound alike, but have different meanings. Find the homophones below. Then write a new sentence for each.

The ancient Egyptians grew **leeks** to eat.

The old faucet **leaks** water.

In the middle of Cairo is a market called the **bazaar.**

The clown wore a **bizarre** hat.

The Past Tense

The past tense shows that an action has already happened. To make the past tense, you usually add "ed" to the end of a verb. Here are some exceptions. Do you know any others?

Today, many Egyptians **wear** T-shirts and jeans.

Long ago, Egyptians **wore** clothing like this.

Today, many Egyptians **build** modern houses.

Long ago, Egyptians **built** pyramids to honor their pharaoh.

Today, people **write** on paper.

Long ago, Egyptians **wrote** on papyrus and stone.

Write About Ancient Egypt

You read about life in ancient Egypt. Now learn more about the ancient Rosetta stone. Who found it? Why was it an important discovery? Where is the stone today?

Research
Collect books and reference materials, or go online.

Read and Take Notes
As you read, take notes and draw pictures.

Write
Write an informational report telling about the Rosetta stone. Include details about who found the stone and where. Also tell who cracked its code and how. Finally, tell where the stone is today.

▶ The Rosetta stone

Read and Compare

Read More About the Ancient Past

Find and read other books about people in the ancient past.
As you read, think about these questions.

- What is special about this ancient culture?
- How was life in ancient times like life today?
- How was it different?

Books to Read

▲ Learn about life in Mexico long ago and today.

▲ Find out more about the people of Egypt, past and present.

▲ Learn about the ancient Inca and their effect on modern Peru.

Glossary

civilization (page 7)
A highly developed culture
Ancient Egypt was home to a great civilization.

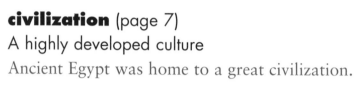

crop (page 9)
A plant that is grown to be used
Ancient Egyptians planted many crops.

mummy (page 15)
A dead body that is treated and wrapped in cloth to make it last a long time
Sometimes a mummy was covered in gold.

pharaoh (page 12)
An ancient Egyptian king
This gold mask was made in honor of a young pharaoh.

pyramid (page 13)
A building with four sides that come together to form a point
Ancient Egyptians built pyramids to honor their pharaohs.

silt (page 8)
A deposit of fresh soil
Silt from the Nile made the land good for farming.

slave (page 12)
A person who is forced to work without pay
The pharaoh had slaves to do his work.

tourism (page 22)
The visiting of a place by people from somewhere else
Tourism brings many people to Egypt every year.

transport (page 18)
A way of moving people or things
Ancient Egyptians used boats as transport.

Index